Waltham Forest Libraries

Please return this item by the last date stamp~
renewed unless required by another

25/04/14	

D0658622

THINGS ABOUT
pregnancy

WALTHAM FOREST LIBRARIES

904 000 00255325

101 amazing
THINGS ABOUT
pregnancy

Afron Monro

CARROLL & BROWN LIMITED

Dedicated to all expectant mums, dads and babies, present and future, and the miracle of new life

First published in 2012 in the United Kingdom by

Carroll & Brown Publishers Limited
20 Lonsdale Road
London NW6 6RD

Managing Art Editor Emily Cook

Text copyright © Afron Monro 2012
Compilation copyright
© Carroll & Brown Limited 2012

A CIP catalogue record for this book
is available from the British Library.

ISBN 978 907952 11 1
10 9 8 7 6 5 4 3 2 1

All rights reserved. No part of this publication may be reproduced in any material form (including photocopying or storing it in any medium by electronic means and whether or not transiently or incidentally to some other use of this publication) without the written permission of the copyright owner, except in accordance with the provisions of the Copyright, Designs and Patents Act of 1988 or under the terms of a licence issued by the Copyright Licensing Agency, 90 Tottenham Court Road, London W1P 9HE. Applications for the copyright owner's written permission to reproduce any part of this publication should be addressed to the publisher.

Waltham Forest Libraries	
904 000 00255325	
Askews & Holts	12-Mar-2013
618.2	£9.99
3821695	

Contents

Foreword

This book is a celebration of the amazing process and feat that is so frequently accomplished; one that is awe-inspiring yet often taken for granted as a part of everyday life. Pregnancy is something that countless women in all cultures and eras have experienced, but for each individual woman, it is entirely new. What happens during these nine months, despite some differences, has given rise to the roots of numerous shared beliefs, rituals and structures.

My wish in writing this book is to offer a glimpse of some of the less well-known aspects of pregnancy – from the microscopic to the societal level – and all that lies in-between; the transforming of a single cell into a communicating, sentient member of humanity. Along the way, I hope these glimpses transform what can be seen as inevitable and even mechanistic into something truly fantastic.

During my training as a midwife, I had a growing sense of awe as I started to recognise how complex and intricate were the workings of conception, pregnancy and birth. It seemed there were so many synchronous changes needed, each crucial, that it was a miracle that it ever worked! As my midwifery career progressed, I gained experience and further understanding in a variety of settings. This was augmented through training and practising as a teacher of

Birthlight perinatal and baby yoga. I began to see, first hand, that the miracle that was set up to work so well had a better chance of fulfilling its potential if it could be supported by the dispelling of misbeliefs and more access to good resources. This was true for both individuals and society as a whole.

The experience of my own journey to motherhood resulted in a deeper awe and understanding, and led to an increase in my interest in new areas of research relating to childbearing and fetal origins. I began to comprehend a very different picture of pregnancy and the newborn from the one that is so often portrayed. With this came the realisation that a gulf existed between the significant information that researchers provide and the understanding that many women have. In so many ways, pregnancy, childbirth and newborns are much more miraculous than we can possibly conceive. So, in the spirit of celebrating the many truly amazing things about having a baby, I hope my book will serve as an eye-opener for all those embarked on a pregnancy, about to embark on one, or cheering one on from the sidelines.

But before you begin to discover today's truths about pregnancy and fetal origins, some of what was believed before (and may still prevail in certain quarters), will show you have much we have learned.

'You can't get pregnant the first time you have sex.'
You can.

'Don't worry about your diet when trying to conceive – it makes no difference.'
This is incorrect in two ways. Lack of essential vitamins and minerals in both men and women reduce their chances of conceiving. For the person being conceived, the amount of good nutrients his mother's body has in it at the time of his conception and in the first weeks of pregnancy makes a huge difference.

'You can tangle the baby's umbilical cord if you raise both arms above your head.'
There is no evidence for this.

'A woman can't get pregnant unless she has an orgasm.'

Although an orgasm helps by sweeping the sperm in the right direction, it is not necessary for the release of a woman's egg or for a pregnancy to start.

'If you get lots of heartburn your baby will be born with a full head of hair.'

There is no evidence to support any connection between heartburn and quantity of hair.

'You'll loose a tooth for every baby.'

Luckily this is not true. Extra care of the gums and teeth is advised during pregnancy as they can be temporarily affected by hormones but a full set of teeth can be kept through many pregnancies with care and a good diet!

01 Trying to influence conception is a universal practice

Both men and women have attempted to avoid or promote conception at different times, whether for financial, health or other reasons; in ancient Egypt and Babylonia, the timing of conception was believed to influence character, fortune and life span.

Probably the most universally used practice to avoid pregnancy is abstinence; references to it appear in Iron Age Indian Vedic scriptures and knowledge of its effectiveness have been found in many tribes.

Practices used to increase the chances of conception included throwing rice at weddings, using particular herbs, praying to fertility goddesses and even decking

The throwing of confetti
at weddings comes
from the older tradition
of throwing rice to
increase fertility.

Conception

trees by sacred springs with 'clooties' (rags) torn from underwear in the hope of a baby.

Currently, people seek to ensure conception using lifestyle changes such as stopping drinking, special diets, avoiding known hazards, and trying recommended sexual positions. Some take drugs for years or undergo operations to both increase or decrease fertility, while others rely on devices and practices that signal the best time to have sex in order to hasten or avoid conception.

02 Sex can be over in minutes yet the results can last for decades

In just two minutes, it's possible to start a pregnancy and decades of life; to date, the oldest person lived for 115 years.

Those shared minutes also can start a process that impacts over many generations – depending on the person being conceived. Florence Nightingale (1820–1910), for example, founded the modern nursing profession with its awareness of the need for sanitation, and this is reflected still in the nursing and midwifery care practised today.

Generally, people affect the future by having children themselves and passing down their genes through the generations.

03 ...and result in beings with vast potential

At birth, a baby has already done an astonishing amount of adapting to his environment, and has an astounding ability to continue to adapt; babies live in both the Arctic and the Sahara, for example, and can even change from one extreme to the other utilising lifestyle and body changes.

Every time we learn to do something new – read music, row a boat or even change a nappy – our brain, and often our body, changes in response to what is required, growing new neural pathways and adding or reducing muscle bulk.

Although we maintain this flexibility throughout life, babies are exceptionally adaptable to different environments.

Conception

04 The desire to influence and predict the gender of a baby is widespread

Down the ages, parents have been passionate about the sex of their baby. In the past, all sorts of actions were tried to produce a baby of a particular gender: men in ancient Greece often had a testicle tied up believing the left testicle to produce girls and the right boys. Others believed a child's gender could be influenced during pregnancy, so that, in certain parts of India, if a pregnant woman used her left foot to cross through a doorway, her baby would be a girl and if the right, a boy.

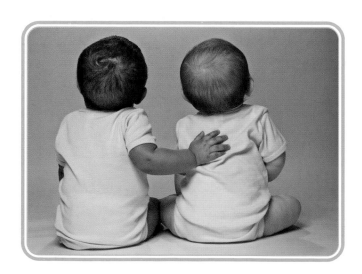

Some folklore traditions still persist: Hungarians may sprinkle poppy seeds on the window sill for a boy and sugar for a girl.

Today, with the development of ultrasound imaging, it is considered normal in many countries to be able to find out the sex of one's baby before he or she is born. Moreover, advances in technology have made it possible to 'create' a child of a particular gender, although this raises moral and ethical questions.

The genetic sex of a child is determined at conception, by information carried in the sperm. By the end of the third month in the womb, there is a recognisable difference between male, female and intersex genitalia (approximately 1 in 1000 babies).

05 Sperm have incredible speed

Sperm come equipped with 'mini power plants' and 'energy production lines' to fuel their fast swimming. Relative to body length, they swim at about one and a half times the speed that Frenchman Alain Bernard did when he broke the world record in the 100m freestyle swim in 2008. He swam 100 metres in 47.6 seconds.

06 ...and they mature through using it

When sperm are ejaculated they are not fully mature. It is only through swimming to the egg that they develop completely. This last bit of growing up equips them with the necessary paraphernalia to join with the egg and release their DNA into it.

07 Sperm can live longer than most people believe (which can make a considerable difference later on)

Reproductive physiologist, Dr Joanna Ellington, has found that particularly healthy sperm can live for over seven days, rather than two to five days as previously believed, when they are kept close to cells from the Fallopian tube. It seems these Fallopian tube cells help sperm to attain longevity, which increases the chances of a conception.

Where a baby's due date, worked out by ultrasound scan, does not appear to match with the mother's knowledge of her dates, this may be explained by such 'enduring' sperm. For example, a woman who has sex with her husband when he is home for just one night may not conceive until a whole week after he goes away again!

The calculated due date can make a big difference to the type of care a woman and her baby receive at the end of pregnancy. Some women, induced for going over their due date, have babies who are afterwards judged to have been born early.

08 Released eggs float in space

The ovaries, where the eggs are stored, and the Fallopian tubes that lead from them to the womb, are not actually attached. When an egg is released from an ovary, it has to float 'through space' to get to the Fallopian tube. The end of the Fallopian tube helpfully moves closer to the egg in order to 'catch' it at this time.

09 An egg can be fertilised by two sperm (with unfortunate results)

When an egg and sperm join, an electrical charge occurs and the stored calcium within the egg is mobilised to strengthen the egg's outer surface. This reaction starts at the entry point of the sperm and spreads around the cell's entire wall, making the wall harder and more protective. The resulting calcium 'barrier' reduces the chances of other sperm getting in and producing a fertilised egg with an extra half set of chromosomes (a condition known as polyspermy). If such a pregnancy occurs, it usually ends in miscarriage although there has been one recently documented case in the UK, where the affected baby was carried and lived after birth.

It is believed as many as half of early miscarriages happen because of chromosomal abnormalities and that polyspermy is among the most common.

10 Both sperm and the fertilised egg are welcomed with easy access and refreshments

Just before and during ovulation, the usually tightly knotted fibres of the cervical mucus at the entrance to the womb loosen and line up to help sperm pass through. The 'hospitality' continues in the form of a nutrient-rich growth-stimulating drink, as the first complete cell of a new human being wafts down the Fallopian tube to the womb. This drink continues to be provided by the womb for about eight weeks until the baby's blood supply is sufficiently advanced.

A freshly fertilised egg passes down the Fallopian tube on its way to implantation in the wall of the womb.

Conception

11 It is possible to carry twins with different dads

Non-identical twins can be conceived naturally if a woman's body releases two eggs at the same time. The tendency to do this can run in families.

If two eggs are released, and the woman has sex with two different men around this time, each egg can be fertilised by a sperm from a different man, thus producing babies of different parentage. This has been known to happen occasionally.

12 Creating a new human being requires a lot of hormones

Producing a baby from start to finish arguably involves every human hormone – those needed for normal day-to-day living as well as the handful that circulate only during pregnancy. At least 15 different hormones are required just to produce the sperm and egg.

Not only is the number of involved hormones extensive but also the quantity of particular ones: oestriol (a type of oestrogen), for example, increases 1000 fold.

Hormones circulate in the blood and other fluids acting as a communication system within the body. They change the actions of specific organs or cells – but only if these have appropriate 'landing platforms'. Depending on what is required, however, cells can change their makeup. Just before labour, for instance, the cells of the womb make lots of 'landing platforms' for the hormone oxytocin (which signals the womb to contract).

13 Within hours of conception, a woman's body changes

Just 24 to 48 hours after an egg has been fertilised, the small ball of cells, or morula, that will develop into her baby, releases a chemical that can be detected in her blood. This chemical slightly suppresses the newly pregnant woman's immune system and helps to stop her body from recognising the new cells of her baby as different from her own.

14 ...and her emotional reactions can be varied in the extreme

Culture and social status strongly influence how a woman is likely to feel about her pregnancy and will affect her beliefs and expectations of what she will experience and what is expected of her. Her reaction can involve the full range of emotions reaching from disbelief to euphoric delight or from fear to relief and anything in between. Many women report that finding out they are pregnant is a deeply emotional experience and takes days to assimilate, as the full implications percolate through.

Woman often feel a pregnancy brings the need for decisions and changes – from what to eat to their relationships with their family, which is partly why it can be such an emotional experience. Interestingly, while there is great variety in the implications pregnancy has for individuals and the emotions they experience, the biology is very similar in all.

15 The time of greatest change often passes unnoticed

In the first three months, a pregnant woman's body experiences enormous changes due to a new and powerful cocktail of hormones.

Most of the changes can't be seen from the outside and the pregnancy can go unnoticed – sometimes even by the woman herself.

Muscles and ligaments stretch, enabling the lower ribs to expand (long before a baby grows big enough to reach them).

The womb grows most of the extra cells it will need to get bigger and it moves out of the pelvis and into the upright position required during pregnancy.

The heart beats faster and the blood changes in chemical make up, volume and pressure.

New levels are set in the brain to
increase the lungs' sensitivity to
carbon dioxide, the amount of fat laid
down and the amount of water
retained. (These changes may be
noticed as feelings of breathlessness
and increased appetite and thirst).

The digestive system
slows down but
becomes more efficient
at drawing out nutrients
from food.

Blood flow to the
kidneys increases by
as much as 50% to
support their extra work.

The emotions and one's state of
mind fluctuate more — even without being
aware of the pregnancy.

16 Pregnancy is the only time when two people inhabit one body

Although there is a division between a mum's body and that of her baby, they are both entirely within the mum's body.

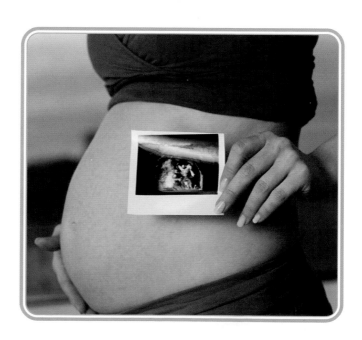

17 A pregnant woman also carries the 'seeds' of any grandchildren

A woman pregnant with a daughter carries cells within her body that could turn into her potential grandchildren in many years' time. By about the sixth week of pregnancy, a developing female baby starts to form her ova (eggs) and by the fifth month of pregnancy,

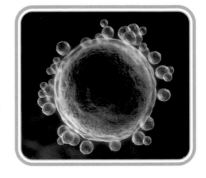

A stylised view of an ovum.

all six to seven million eggs are fully formed and stored for puberty.

A woman, pregnant with a son, carries the cells from which his sperm will be made (a process that starts at puberty), so although these cells are the foreunners, they are not the exact cells that would form the next generation.

18 A mum's body becomes soft and stretchy

From early in pregnancy, levels of 'stretch' hormones rise, increasing dramatically in the weeks before birth and continuing, to a lesser degree, the whole time she breastfeeds. Although these hormones are very effective for the areas that need loosening — such as the hips, belly and ribs — they also affect the rest of the body, so it becomes easier for women to overextend themselves and damage muscles and ligaments. Therefore, it's important not to push the body during exercise, although this can be challenging for women used to working out vigorously.

19 Her blood supply is separate from her baby's – but only just

The division between the two circulations is so tiny – thinner than a hair – that it is common for mothers to have a few of their baby's blood cells in their own blood. All the food and oxygen from the mother's blood passes through these layers.

Ordinarily a small mixing of mum's and baby's blood does not cause a problem, but occasionally it can. A mother's blood is either Rhesus positive or Rhesus negative. The smaller proportion of women whose blood type is Rhesus negative can develop antibodies against a baby who has a Rhesus positive blood type. Usually this only causes problems in a subsequent pregnancy and can be avoided if mum is given a medicine called anti-D after any occasion that is likely to have caused mum's and baby's blood to mix in larger amounts, such as a miscarriage, a fall or when giving birth.

20 A pregnant woman's heart pumps twice its normal amount of blood

To keep pace with her growing baby and her own bodily changes, the amount of blood pumped around a woman's body as much as doubles during pregnancy. Most of this increase is attained in the first half of pregnancy and is caused by the heart beating faster and pushing out more blood with each beat. A baby needs a good supply of blood; by the end of pregnancy, almost a fifth of a mother's blood goes to her womb. Some of this is for the womb itself but the majority goes to the baby and his placenta.

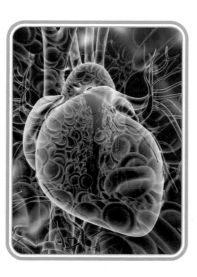

A pregnant woman's heart must beat faster and push out more blood with each beat.

21 ...and helps to keep her baby's heart beating

The rhythmic pulsing of the heart muscle is coordinated by an electrical charge that moves through it with every heartbeat. The electromagnetic field created by this electricity has an amplitude 60 times greater than brain waves.

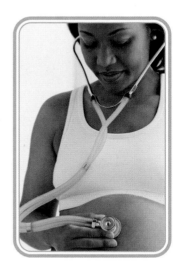

Just as brain waves change with different states of mind, so, too, are the heart waves affected by different emotions and, as confirmed by Rollin McCraty, Director of Research at the HeartMath Institute, they carry this information with them.

The adult heart emits three measurable electromagnetic fields, with the most expansive detectable at a distance of four metres away. These electromagnetic pulses support and encourage other heart muscle to contract rhythmically. A baby enjoys being bathed in the closest field of her mother's electromagnetic heart waves during her entire time in the womb.

22 A mum's love and good times help protect her unborn baby from stress

Among the hormones a woman produces and which can cross over from her body to her baby's body are cortisol and oxytocin. Cortisol is connected with ongoing stress; high levels can cause health problems for unborn babies, especially in the first three months of pregnancy. Oxytocin, on the other hand, is connected with loving, peaceful and contented feelings; it reduces the harmful effects of cortisol by acting directly on it.

According to Professor Kerstin Uvnas Moberg of the Karolinska Institute in Stockholm, oxytocin, often called 'the hormone of love', is released when someone feels love, does something fun, shares intimately or just enjoys a nice meal in good company. In other words, having loving and supportive friends or family around can help to keep a pregnant woman's cortisol at normal levels. Even having one trusted friend to talk to during pregnancy has been shown to reduce anxiety levels significantly.

Many women find that yoga exercises, designed for pregnancy, are also effective for increasing feelings of

peace and wellbeing. Indeed, studies show that practising yoga leads to an increased release of oxytocin. Relaxation is thought to be a large part of this and it is well known that even simple relaxation techniques, used regularly, can have dramatic effects, including reducing the risk of giving birth prematurely.

Although difficult and stressful things can happen at any time, and sometimes can not be avoided or put off, a woman can draw on her body's own medicine cupboard to counteract their negative effects.

23 The pituitary gland more than doubles in size during pregnancy

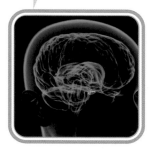

Located near the front of the brain, the pituitary gland produces several hormones including oxytocin, which causes contractions, and prolactin, which signals the breasts to make milk. During pregnancy, the gland increases in weight by 135%.

In various traditions, the pituitary gland is linked to a sixth sense, which may account for the reputed 'mother's intuition'.

The Pregnant Mum (and Dad)

24 Breasts are ready for feeding a baby at 14 weeks after conception

Women usually notice their breasts changing early on in pregnancy; tingling sensations, itchiness and tenderness are caused by the conversion of the breasts into providers of sustenance. The cells in the breasts change and multiply on a grand scale, creating milk ducts and increasing the blood supply. Early on in the second trimester, they are able to express colostrum (first milk). Women who have been pregnant before often find this happens even earlier and that the colostrum does not always stay in the breasts!

25 A pregnant woman carries far greater extra weight than that of her baby

It is estimated that in the average pregnancy, only about 25% of weight gained can be attributed to the baby while a further 11% is due to the weight of the placenta and the waters around the baby. The other 64% is made up of the increased weight of the womb and other maternal organs, muscles and fat, and the extra six to eight litres of fluid retained in-between cells and in the blood.

The recommended weight gain during pregnancy ranges from 11–16 kilogrammes, depending on a woman's pre-pregnancy weight; this is comparable to her carrying between 18 and 26 pints of milk everywhere she goes.

26 ... but baby's growth can be overwhelming

Between 20 and 24 weeks of pregnancy, babies experience a huge growth spurt, and double in weight. To keep up with a baby's increased weight and size and the extra work and stretching her body is called on to produce, a mother's body has to make a 'leap'. The pregnancy becomes much more visible – the woman tending to feel her tummy is stretched to its limit – and her hip joints and lower back ache. Over time, any aches or feelings of over-stretch usually ease as the body adjusts.

The Pregnant Mum (and Dad)

27 Brains go 'funny' during pregnancy

Most women find that when pregnant, they become forgetful and have a hunger for spending more time 'doing nothing' or daydreaming. For women who have

high-powered jobs or are used to being busy, this can be challenging. But 'doing nothing' facilitates a stronger connection with the baby and a deeper assimilation of current changes and those to come.

Forgetfulness and turning inwards tend to increase as a pregnancy grows and are the result of pregnancy hormones. Embracing this state by spending more time 'doing nothing' makes for an easier transition to motherhood.

Women often find these hormonal effects on the brain tricky for keeping things organised, though they are beneficial in more ways than the ones mentioned above. They also enable the increased ability to relax effectively, so that if a pregnant woman engages in deep relaxation on a regular basis, she will benefit from a healthier body, clearer mind and steadier emotions. Teachers of relaxation techniques are often surprised how easily pregnant women master these techniques, compared to other people.

28 Dads get 'pregnant', too

In many tribal societies, it has long been the case that men experience or act out what their pregnant or labouring partners experience. Until recently, this 'couvade syndrome' was thought to be a ritualistic act only. However, various studies have found that a surprising number of Western men experience symptoms similar to their pregnant partner. These range from weight increase and nausea, through to enlarged breasts and sizeable growth of the stomach.

29 Even during pregnancy, a father can make a big difference to his child's health and intelligence

A number of studies have shown that babies in utero are affected by stress; the most negative effects usually result from their parents' relationship difficulties. Therefore, if a man is a supportive and understanding partner, this can bring health benefits to his baby such as increased weight gain and a reduced risk of premature birth.

Research further shows that dads who are more involved during pregnancy spend significantly more time with their babies after they are born. The National Fatherhood Initiative in America has collected research showing that dads who give more hands-on care raise children with increased cognitive and emotional intelligence.

Dads say that listening to their baby's heartbeat, seeing their baby at an ultrasound scan or buying something for baby, makes them feel more involved. Some dads like to talk and sing to their baby, or gently massage their baby through their partner's belly and will often find baby responds with movements.

The Pregnant Mum (and Dad)

30 Life in the womb affects all that follows

There is growing research evidence that links the womb environment with a baby's later temperament as well as his physical, mental and emotional health and abilities. According to Vivette Glover, Professor of

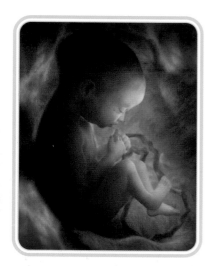

Perinatal Psychobiology at Imperial College, London, the surrounding environment of the womb has a greater impact on a person than any other environment.

There are two avenues that help to explain the phenomenon. The first is that the womb environment acts directly on a baby as he forms. In other words, it contains the building material that is available for a baby's body and the means that enable him to experience the world in which he will be born.

The second is explained by the fast-growing science of epigenetics, which looks at changes to the way in which a person's genes are used rather than a change in the structure of one's DNA.

Every person has roughly 25,000 genes that carry his or her genetic information but only some are active; the rest remain dormant with no evidence that they even exist. Which genes are 'switched' on or off has been found to be a result of chemicals made in the body and from the environment. This could mean, for example, that something his mother ate during pregnancy determined which gene was used for an individual's hair colour (red or blond), or gave him good life-long protection from cancer.

Throughout a person's life, factors such as food and air quality continue to determine which genes are activated or left dormant, but their effects are particularly significant while a baby is developing in the womb.

31 Many of us started out with a twin

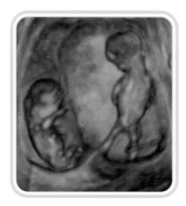

These twins at 11 weeks' gestation continued to develop in the uterus and both were born alive.

It is believed that as many as one in eight pregnancies start out with twins (or more) but that early in the pregnancy, one is miscarried or reabsorbed. This is known as 'vanishing twin syndrome', because if a tiny baby is reabsorbed, she disappears without trace.

Psychologists recognise that losing a twin while in the womb can be the cause of some people suffering from an unexplained sense of loss or 'something missing'. Some talking and body therapies, and others, such as Family Constellations Therapy, which could be called more of a soul therapy, have been found to put such feelings to rest.

32 Mother and baby work together to sustain life

By the sixth or seventh day after conception, when the forming baby (known as a blastocyst) starts to need more sustenance to continue life, chemical changes occur that enable it to attach to her mother's womb: the womb produces a substance, which dissolves the very outer layer of the blastocyst and the blastocyst makes another that helps to break down the lining of the womb. Over the following days the forming baby becomes enveloped in the womb lining and a direct blood supply is set up.

This process of attachment can cause a small blood loss (which normally occurs around 28 days after a woman's last menstrual period), that is often mistaken for a light period.

A stylised cellular view of a blastocyst.

33 The placenta organises a baby's body

This incredible organ develops more from the genetic instructions 'given' by the dad rather than the mum. Among the numerous essential jobs the placenta does, it makes some 36 chemicals, which are needed for a baby's healthy growth. One of their purposes is to literally organise which cells turn into which part of the baby.

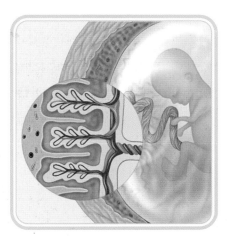

Shown in close-up, you can see that the placental walls are rich in nourishing blood vessels.

34 ...and acts like a radiator

While a baby is in the womb he is always warmer than his mother because all the growing he does continuously produces heat. The placenta keeps him cool (and mum extra warm) by transmitting the heat he makes out into his mother's body – just like a car radiator serves to keep an engine cool and warms the air around it.

35 The placenta ensures babies benefit from their mother's antibodies

Special carriers in the placenta take antibodies from a mother's blood to her baby. They work so well that at birth babies often have twice as many antibodies in their blood as their mother. This helps to give them protection from diseases, which their mother has either developed antibodies for naturally or through being vaccinated.

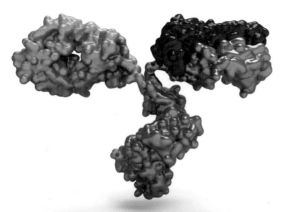

Immunoglobulin G antibody molecule. This is the most abundant immunoglobulin and is found in all body fluids.

36 To keep a pregnancy going, there is a delicate change over from mother to baby

Pregnancy is orchestrated by specific quantities of specific hormones; without these, pregnancy cannot progress. During the first weeks, part of the mother's ovary makes the hormones that maintain pregnancy. But between 12 and 14 weeks after conception, this function becomes the responsibility of the placenta. This change over is delicate, making this a sensitive time for pregnancy and one of the most common times for the baby to miscarry. This is why women are often advised to take it easy during this phase of pregnancy.

37 The umbilical cord has built-in protective cushioning

The umbilical cord connects a baby to his placenta and effectively works as his lifeline, bringing him oxygen and food and removing waste. The cord is about as thick as an adult's thumb and tends to get squashed as a baby gets bigger and during labour. The blood vessels in it are protected by a thick jelly-like substance known as 'Whorton's jelly;' this works so well that even when the baby ties a knot in his cord, the blood flow is protected. A knot can result when a sufficiently small baby passes through a loop in his cord, and is more common with a livelier baby as the more active a baby is, the longer his umbilical cord will grow.

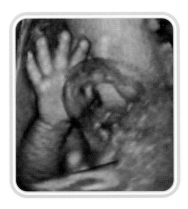

38 The waters surrounding the baby are continually renewed

Amniotic fluid needs constant replacing, which involves a cooperative effort between the mother's body, the baby's body and the placenta

and surrounding membranes. Fluid volume is at its greatest during the middle of pregnancy, when there is an average turnover of 1000 millilitres per day – the equivalent of four mugs of water being moved in and four mugs of water being moved out from around the baby every 24 hours, or two eggcups of water on the move every hour. By term, the amount of new liquid produced is smaller but it is still enough to cause continual leaking once the waters have broken.

39 A person's biggest growth spurt occurs in the first weeks following conception

The largest relative growth that any human ever experiences in a matter of weeks happens at the very beginning of his or her existence. In just nine weeks, a developing human grows from a single 0.1 centimetre cell to a 2–3 centimetre-long fetus with all organs and limbs present. Some of the organs are in a basic form, but the face is recognisably human, and 10 fingers and toes are present. Even after all this growth, at over nine weeks of age, a developing baby is still tiny – more than 50 times smaller than the average adult.

40 Within days of being a single cell, a developing baby's heart begins to beat

A baby's heart begins to beat just 22 to 23 days after his egg and sperm have fused together. The heart is a part of his cardiovascular system, the first major body system to start working.

41 Early in their gestation, babies have a tail

At about 20 days after conception a baby has a small tail and by the time he is 26 days old, his tail is almost as long as the rest of his body. The cells from his tail then migrate and are used to form other parts of his body. By the time he is 56 days old, his tail has largely disappeared so when he is born, he is tail-less except for the tail bone (coccyx) at the end of his spine.

The mass of cells known as a blastocyst elongates to form a head and tail, which gives the developing baby a tadpole-like appearance.

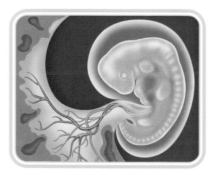

42 ...and webbed fingers and toes

Fingers and toes start out fused in the womb, but within days they become separate digits. Webbed fingers can be seen by 41 days after conception, toes at 44 days.

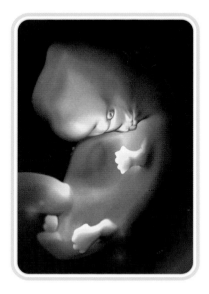

As the digits grow and lengthen, the cells making up the webbing adhere to their pre-programming and die, leaving the fingers free by 52 days, and the toes by 54 days after conception.

43 Touch is the first sense to develop

Just six weeks after being conceived, babies can respond to stimulation. When they are touched on the lips they move. It is possible that a baby even younger can respond to stimulation but as of yet, we do not have the tools to measure this.

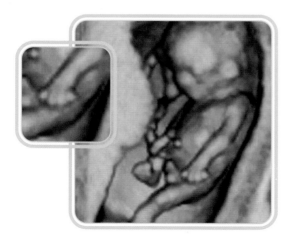

At 11 weeks' gestation, this baby's opposable thumbs have formed. They will be vital in enabling her to pick up, hold and manipulate items both in the womb and beyond.

44 Pheromone-like chemicals guide growing nerves

In order to be able to feel and move, a body needs nerves to conduct electrical signals from one part to another. In a developing baby, nerves start forming in a specific place and grow their way to where they need to connect. To make sure that the growing nerves reach their correct destinations, the 'landing points' secrete chemical molecules similar to pheromones. These move outward from the spot producing them and attract the nerve ending.

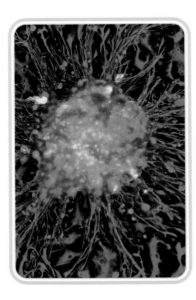

A neural stem cell is differentiating into neurons (red) and nerve support cells (green), which are migrating away.

45 Babies in utero move long before their mothers can feel them

A first-time mother typically becomes aware of her baby's movements between 18 and 22 weeks of pregnancy. If, from a previous pregnancy, a woman is familiar with the feeling of a baby touching the inside of her womb, she may become aware of the sensation earlier, at about 16 weeks of pregnancy.

Yet a baby has enough 'bones', ligaments, muscles and nerves to move at just six weeks of age. His first movements are jerks and twitches of the limbs and trunk. By eight weeks of age, he is able to make his first controlled movement, which is a slow stretching of the back of his neck by pushing the top of his head away from the rest of his body and tucking his chin in at the same time. This is followed within a matter of days by controlled movements of his arms and legs.

46 ... and engage in recognisable behaviour

A developing baby, only nine weeks after conception, can make familiar movements like yawning and hiccupping and a week or two later can actually suck her thumb.

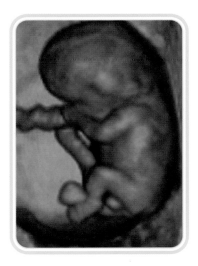

47 Babies practise breathing in the womb

From the sixth month of life in the womb, babies frequently make rhythmic breathing movements sucking the waters surrounding them in and out of their lungs. This strengthens their breathing muscles in preparation for their first momentous breath.

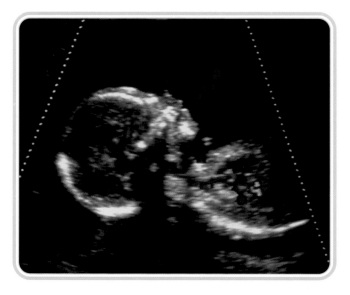

Doppler ultrasound that shows amniotic fluid (red patches) flowing out of a baby's mouth as he makes breathing movements. Such movements stimulate normal lung growth and the secretion of a lung cell coating.

48 A baby's world is made up of his mother's internal and external environment

Internal influences affecting a baby include the waters in which he is cushioned; the inside of the womb, with which he comes into contact; and his mother's body, which encircles him, as well as the sound of her heartbeat, and the actions of

the hormones and other chemicals her body makes. These, in turn, are affected by her surroundings and the way she feels about them.

The external influences on a baby's environment come from his mother's surroundings, for example, the air she breathes and the vibrations from the vehicles in which she travels. These are like little 'memos' sent to inform him about the world into which he will be born.

The baby, too, can produce chemicals or actions that affect his mother and hence her environment. For instance, he can move so vigorously that his mum stops what she is doing. Sometimes these are reactions to stimuli that have come into baby's world – like hearing loud music.

Life in Utero

49 A mother's emotions can alter the structural design of her baby's brain

When a baby's mother feels threatened, fearful or unsupported, more blood is provided for the baby's developing hindbrain, which is reactive, defensive and instinctual, and plays a key role in self-protection. If a mother experiences these feelings over a sustained period of time, her baby's hindbrain becomes more fully developed at the expense of his forebrain. In other words, a baby's survival instincts and reflex reactions are prioritised over conscious thought, reasoning and creativity.

50 A developing baby's hearing is surprisingly acute

During his last months in the womb, a baby is continually bathed in sound from his immediate environment, his mother's body and beyond, and at a level of background noise many adults are used to. Hearing starts at around 24 weeks of age but takes time to develop fully. Professor Jean-Pierre Lecanuet, of the French National Centre for Scientific Research, explains that in the third trimester, despite the muffling effect of his environment, a baby's hearing has become so good that he is able to distinguish between slight changes in pitch and rhythm. He can even tell the difference between a live voice and a recorded one.

It was only around 100 years ago that scientists started to consider whether babies might hear in the womb, even though mothers and fathers have talked and sung to their unborn babies since time immemorial, often using rhymes and songs traditionally created for this purpose.

Life in Utero

51 A baby can 'dance' to her mother's voice

Professors William Cordon and Lewis Sanders of Boston University discovered that babies move precise muscles or groups of muscles to the phonemes (smallest parts making up verbal language) in their mother's speech. These are so predictable that the researchers could plot the movements a baby would make to a particular sentence – before the sentence was spoken.

This ability develops in the last months in the womb and carries on after birth. A slowed-down video of a newborn listening to her mother's voice shows her moving to it in a similar way to the way a child or adult moves when dancing freely to music.

52 ... and swim and somersault in the womb

During the second trimester, babies spend much of their wakeful time moving about and turning over, often using the inside of the womb to propel themselves. This activity is essential for muscles to develop and to wire up all the nerves that send messages to, from and within their body and brain.

53 A baby's world is filled with flavours and aromas

When a mother digests her food, certain molecules that cause taste and smell enter her blood stream, and

from there they can get into the waters in which her developing baby floats.

Evidence has been found by Martin Witt and colleagues of the Technical College of Dresden, Germany, that babies may be able to taste as early as their 14th week in the womb. It is clear that not much later than this they can detect and discriminate between the four main tastes: sweet, sour, bitter and salty. Their favourite is sweet!

Although the smelling mechanisms develop much earlier, babies don't sense smell until their sixth month in the womb because their nostrils are blocked until then. Once the waters can move into the nostrils they bring aromatic molecules to the smell receptors in the same way that air does for an adult.

Life in Utero

54 Babies smile in the womb

The age at which a baby starts to smile has been a controversial issue for decades, with some people adamant that a baby can smile at two weeks after birth, others saying it can only happen when the baby is several weeks older. Now, with new developments in technology, it is possible to watch the facial expressions that a baby makes before she is even born. In the second half of pregnancy babies make different faces – smiling, scowling and sticking their tongue out.

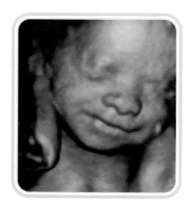

55 The first memories are laid down in the womb

Many studies have shown that voices, movements, tastes and pieces of music can be remembered by babies while they are in the womb and still recognised shortly after birth. There is also compelling evidence of children, and roughly 1% of adults, being able to remember consciously their birth or even pre-birth. It seems to be quite a common thing for children under six years of age to remember their birth and be able to communicate this through words or through replicating the movements their body made.

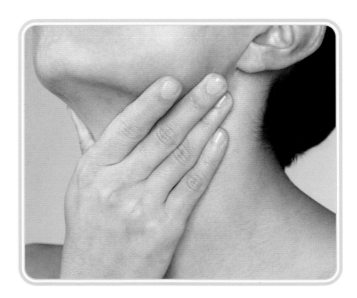

Dr. Ludwig Janus, president of the International Society of Prenatal and Perinatal Psychology and Medicine for many years, confirms that there is a large body of anecdotal evidence where adults have accessed memories of womb life in great detail through various techniques employed in a range of therapies. Although the workings of this are not yet fully understood, there is evidence suggesting some of these memories are stored in a form known as 'somatic' or 'biological memory'. This is connected to an event that involved a particular part of the body, such as a baby's neck being constricted by a tightly wrapped umbilical cord. This memory, or feelings associated with it, may be evoked later when the area is touched.

Frequently, a baby will try to avoid re-experiencing an unpleasant birth sensation by moving away from being touched or 'fighting' it off. This often seemingly inexplicable dislike can persist right into adulthood.

56 Babies respond to their mother's thoughts

Babies in the womb are sensitive to emotions in their mother's voice and even to their mother's thoughts. Experiments done by researcher Marie-Claire Busnel and her colleagues of the French National Centre for Scientific Research, showed that babies in their second trimester reacted to their mother thinking about them. In fact, they could even tell the difference between their mother thinking about them and her 'talking' in her head to them. For example, when a mother switched from thinking about the day's news to wondering how her baby was doing, her baby's heartbeat registered more excitement. If the mother then began to say in her head "How are you today? I hope you are happy in there..." her baby's heartbeat (using cardiotocography or CTG) showed signs of an even more alert state.

57 Babies produce the 'best barrier cream ever'

While a baby is in the womb and surrounded by water, her skin needs to be protected from becoming waterlogged. This is done with vernix caseosa — a thick, greasy, white 'cream' that covers a baby's skin for much of her time in the womb. Towards the end of pregnancy, there is less of it and often by the time a baby is born, it can only be found in creases such as the inside of the elbow. Therefore, if a baby is born a little early, she is likely to be covered in it and if she is born late, there may be none to see at all.

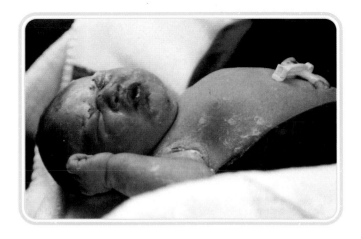

58 Twins start their relationship patterns in the womb

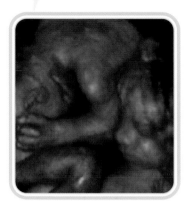

The development of real-time ultrasound has made it possible to watch movements in the womb as they happen. Using this technology, psychologist Alessandra Piontelli and her co-workers confirm that twins develop their own particular pattern of communication, sometimes starting as early as their third month in the womb. There is evidence that these patterns of relating continue into infancy and beyond.

An example of such studied behaviour patterns is where one twin reached out his hand to touch his twin's face through their dividing membrane. His sister would then respond by turning towards him and they would gently touch cheeks. At one year old, a favourite game of this set of twins, was to re-enact this pattern of interaction with a curtain separating them.

Life in Utero

59 No two babies are ever exactly the same

Even identical twins are not truly identical; they always have their own unique fingerprints. These start to form already in their tenth week in utero.

During their time in the womb, twins will have different experiences. A particular part of one twin may become squashed as he grows or his blood supply may be greater or less than his sibling. Such situations can cause changes ranging from different genes being switched on or off (see item 12) and slight variations in brain make-up, to notable differences in weight and character. Differences at birth tend to impact on how twins interact with their environment, which results in still greater differences as time goes by.

60 At birth, a baby is completely primed for the exact environment he will inhabit

During pregnancy, a baby becomes intimate with his mother's world. His senses of smell, taste, touch and hearing are finely tuned to what is going on around him and, once born, serve to guide him to the safety of familiarity. He knows the smell of his family's food, washing powder and toiletries. His mother's milk tastes of the flavours he encountered in the waters that surrounded him in the womb. He recognises his parents' voices and the usual noises in the home and outdoors and will be comforted by the rocking movements of his mother walking, similar to those he experienced while in the womb.

61 The longest pregnancy outside a womb lasted 33 weeks

Maria Hoey of Belfast, Northern Ireland had the longest recorded ectopic pregnancy. Her son was born by caesarean section after 233 days.

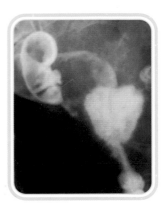

An ectopic pregnancy is when a fertilised egg attaches somewhere other than inside the womb – the most usual place being in the Fallopian tube, which leads from the ovary to the womb. It is believed to occur in about 1 in 100 pregnancies and often ends naturally in miscarriage. Usually, if an ectopic pregnancy continues, strong pain is felt on one side of the lower belly. If not medically ended, it becomes dangerous for the mother and there is a strong likelihood of internal bleeding leading to death. It is possibly the highest cause of loss of life in early pregnancy world wide. In extremely rare cases, however, an ectopic pregnancy can continue until the baby is old enough to be born by surgery.

A 10–12-week-old fetus is developing in the right Fallopian tube. The uterus is the white, heart-shaped mass.

Life in Utero

62 Women have been carrying and birthing their babies successfully for 400,000 years

Every single one of your direct ancestors was carried and birthed successfully. You are the living proof. This awesome capability will have passed life on through times of scarcity and abundance, anxiety and peace.

63 ...though birthing positions go in and out of fashion

Women gave birth standing, kneeling, squatting, sitting in a birthing chair, and on all fours (postures that offer as much as 30% more room for a baby to be born) until the 17th century, when King Louis XIV of France, created a fashion for giving birth lying on one's back. Although this is probably the most uncomfortable birthing position, it enabled him to view his mistresses giving birth, and rapidly became the most widely used.

Today, labouring women are encouraged to move between different positions in order to find the most comfortable ones.

The desire to influence the timing of birth cuts across epochs and ethnic groups

People have resorted to medication, prayer, special diets and surgery to speed up or stall birth. For centuries and on every continent, humans have believed the time of birth shapes a person's fate and

character, depending on things as diverse as the way coins fall and the positions of the planets. Many have tried to influence births to occur at the most 'auspicious' times. There is also a long history of medical attendants at births speeding things up for their own convenience and of course, many births are hastened or suppressed for the sake of the mother's or baby's health.

With the event of the elective caesarean section, women are becoming more casual about having control over the date their baby is born. The bookings for elective caesareans go up and down depending on all sorts of things including festive seasons, school registration dates, and in some countries, even the national identification number the baby would receive.

Women desperate to deliver have tried all sorts of things to bring on the birth from eating pineapple, which contains the enzyme bromelain thought to help soften the cervix, to scrubbing floors, stimulating their nipples or having sex.

65 Mother and baby produce a little pharmacy of analgesics during labour

These help to ease the labour pains for the mother and the likely pains of being squashed and squeezed for the baby. The body's use of it's own natural pain relief is set in motion in response to the pains of labour. Enkephalins, dopamine, oxytocin and endorphins are produced, which act to reduce pain in different ways, some similar to opiates like morphine. Although a baby's bodily system for feeling and dealing with pain during labour is not quite the same as an adult's, it still produces its own pain killers.

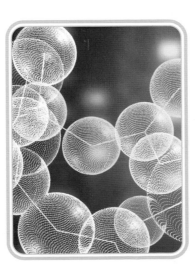

Computer rendering of part of an enkephalin molecule whose effecs resemble those of the drugs morphine and codeine.

Often the simplest things help labour the most

Things that make a woman feel safe promote the release of hormones that make labour swifter, less painful and remembered in a better light. Such things include having a loving partner, trusted friend or doula nearby; being able to choose where labour takes  place, and simply having low lighting and comfort aids such as cushions and favourite snacks, etc.

Frequently changing position and utilising rocking movements or hip circling helps the flow of hormones and can aid the physical mechanics of labour and make it more comfortable. So, too, can relaxing, if not during a contraction then in-between them, and in water. Feeling free to make sounds ('oohs' and 'aahs' are particularly effective later on) is also beneficial.

Disturbance of any kind and having to sort out logistics, such as organising transport to a hospital, tend to slow labour down and, in some cases, even halt it for a while.

Labour and birth

67 The womb muscles prepare for labour early in pregnancy

Although very few women can feel their womb making practice contractions, these start early – even before a pregnancy is visible. All the months of working out result in the muscles of the womb being some of the strongest in the human body.

68 ... and other muscles can help or hinder it

There are muscles in the chest, back, hips and legs that can speed up or slow down labour. Many of these muscles are affected by what a woman does in her normal daily life. Frequent horse riding, for example, can prolong labour because it toughens up the muscles of the perineum, which need to be relaxed and stretchy to let a baby's head be born.

The psoas muscles are two large muscles which sweep down the lower back and though the hips. When these are properly toned, they help a baby to assume a good position in preparation for and during labour. However, the frequent wearing of high heels can shorten them and chronic stress can cause excessive tension in them, which can affect labour adversely. This tension results in an over-accentuated arch in the lower back and the feet turning outwards.

Women naturally assume a similar posture when heavily pregnant, but this is for different reasons and is normal.

Labour and birth

69 Women give birth in all sorts of ways

Many women follow the norm for their time and society, whilst others choose to go a different route.

Women labour and give birth alone (labouring women tend to be drawn to private and protected places, a desire goes back to our most ancient roots) or surrounded by many helpers.

They do so at home, in hospital, in special huts and out in the fields and even in cars, and on trains, planes and boats.

Women give birth feeling agony, ecstasy, anger, love, fear, joy and anticipation.

They give birth naturally or by ventouse, forceps or caesarean section.

They give birth in many positions, pushing or relaxing, onto the earth, into a midwife's hands or into water (both birthing pools and the sea).

They birth babies head, bottom, feet or face first; deliver twins or many more babies – one straight after the other or days apart, spot on their due date or weeks before or after.

70 Some women really do orgasm during giving birth

Much as labour is often experienced as painful, some women really do have ecstatic multiple orgasms while labouring and giving birth. When the natural cascade of hormones is encouraged during labour there is a greater chance of having this experience. Relaxation, feeling safe and having supportive loving people around helps this flow of natural hormones (see item 66). Having medical intervention, even pain relief tends to disrupt it.

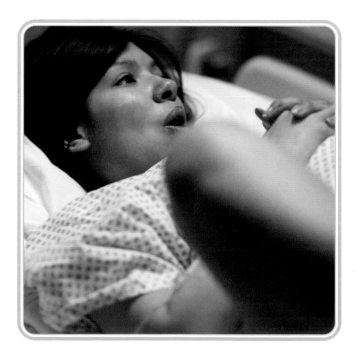

71 ...and some women have spiritual revelations

Occasionally women, even those with no previous spiritual interest, have life-changing spiritual experiences during labour and giving birth. Women have described having had un-doubtable 'inner knowings', of having a connection to something much bigger than themselves, or of being filled with an all-consuming love that is unsurpassed at any other time in their life.

Women can find it difficult to integrate these experiences into their normal daily life, particularly if they live in a culture that does not recognise or validate these. They are often hesitant to talk about them through fear of being misunderstood or thought of as crazy, and find it difficult to put something so powerful into words. Pregnancy and birthing are highly spiritual times in some traditions and these provide a context in which such experiences can be understood.

72 Some women can 'breathe' their baby out

The term 'breathing a baby out' refers to a woman relaxing so much in the second stage of labour (usual pushing stage) that the baby is born just using the effort of the womb contractions without any active pushing. To do this, a woman uses her breath to let the urge to push wash over her, and to relax the muscles in her vagina and perineum. This requires a good amount of body awareness and breath control and is easier in a second or subsequent birth.

A more attainable technique is to be able to keep the vagina and perineum relaxed while bearing down. In other words, to be able to tense some muscles while completely relaxing others. Doing this avoids the unhelpful, exhausting and possibly labour-stalling situation of a woman expending lots of energy pushing her baby with muscles in her upper body against tensed muscles in her lower body.

73 Four babies are born every second

It is estimated that every second, four babies are born somewhere on the planet. These figures will go up and down depending on several factors. When it is night in more densely populated areas of the world, the numbers will go up  as more women naturally go into labour at night. However, this will be partly offset by the countries where a lot of caesarean sections are done, as more of these happen in the day time. The time of year will also influence the numbers as more women have their babies nine months after national holidays, festivals and celebrations.

74 More babies are born by caesarean than ever

Over the last twenty to thirty years, there has been a phenomenal increase in the percentage of babies born this way. Since 1990 the rates in the UK have risen from an estimated 12% to 25%, and in China they have risen even faster – estimated at 5% in the early 1990's to a current 50%. Some countries, such as Brazil with its estimated rate of 70%, have more babies born by caesarean than any other way.

In some circumstances, a caesarean is a life-saving procedure. However, it is clear that the above rates do not reflect this need. Caesarean section carries risks of its own and this is shown by the rates of caesareans in different countries not always reflecting the safety of childbirth there.

Some of the reasons stated for high numbers of caesareans are fear of natural childbirth, fear of litigation by medical staff, previous caesarean delivery and the desire to 'organise' the birth for a particular day in the diary. As there is a tendency for a woman to repeat her own type of birth experience, particularly with her first child, reliance on operative births may rise much higher in future generations.

75 The largest number of babies recorded for one mother is 69

The world record for having the largest number of babies goes to the wife of Feodor Vanilyev (1707–1782), a Russian peasant. She had a recorded total of 69 babies! These arrived as four sets of quadruplets, seven sets of triplets, and the rest as twins during 27 labours.

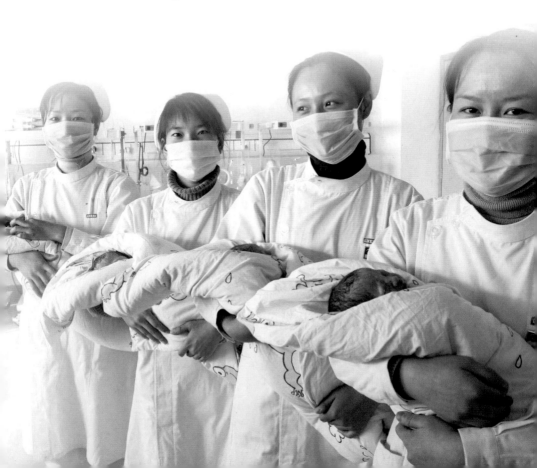

76 The oldest woman to give birth had almost reached her 67th birthday

The verified oldest woman to give birth is Maria del Carmen Bousada Lara at the age of 66 years and 358 days. She had fertility treatment resulting in twin boys delivered by caesarean section in Spain in October 2006. However, the oldest woman on record to conceive naturally is Dawn Brooke of Guernsey. She ovulated past her last period, became pregnant, and had her baby at the age of 59 in 1997 (shortly before she became eligible for her pension).

77 Birth experience explains many things about a person

The fast-evolving science of pre- and perinatal psychology shows growing evidence that a baby's experience of birth has an incredibly formative effect

that reaches right into his adult life. People who have had a gentle, natural birth with a loving welcome, for example, are more likely to have rewarding intimate relationships in life. However, those who have had a traumatic birth are not necessarily destined to have a troubled life. Like everyone, each baby is affected differently by difficult experiences and, as with trauma at any age, it seems it is possible for it to heal. Adults can find various ways of healing these imprints but there are also techniques that help a baby to release the patterns caused by a distressing birth. These often involve skin-to-skin gentle touch, and responding to body and verbal 'baby language' appropriately in the baby's first days and weeks.

Labour and birth

78 Blood vessels in the umbilical cord start to shut down seconds after birth

Coloured scanning electron micrograph showing a blood vessel (purple/red) in the umbilical cord.

Through most of a baby's nine months in the womb, the blood vessels in the umbilical cord carry, without fail, the blood that keeps her alive. Yet, if the umbilical cord is left alone after a normal birth, the arteries that carry blood from the baby to the placenta start to shut down five seconds after birth and are completely closed in just 45 seconds while the vein, which carries oxygenated blood to the baby, begins to close down 15 seconds after birth and is completely closed within three to four minutes. This mechanism encourages the baby to start breathing, provides important extra blood, and helps the placenta to come away from the wall of the womb.

... and the mother's blood supply to the placenta is reduced in a very ingenious way

The 100 or so arteries that carry a mother's blood to the place where the placenta attaches to the womb, need to be closed down quickly after birth. These arteries, rather than growing relatively straight like most arteries in the body, instead spiral through the muscles of the womb. This means that after a normal birth when a woman's body releases a big surge of hormone to make the womb muscles contract strongly, these arteries are squeezed shut far more effectively.

Colour doppler ultrasound shows blood flow through the placenta. The yellow/red area is blood in the two maternal veins on each side of the placenta.

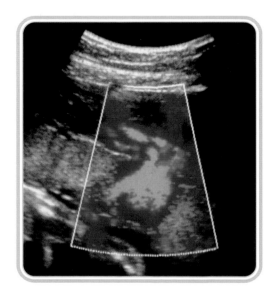

80 A baby's blood flow changes dramatically, too, once he's born

One of the remarkable adjustments that happens in a baby's body at birth is the closing down of a big artery (similar in size to the aorta, the biggest in the body). This is the Ductus arteriosus, which, during life in the womb, provides the route for blood to bypass the lungs. With a baby's first breaths, the muscles of this artery contract, stopping blood using this diversionary route, and ensuring instead that blood continues along the pulmonary artery and thence to the lungs to pick up oxygen. In this way, the amount of blood going to a baby's lungs increases from 10% to almost 100% within a matter of minutes.

81 ...and to make breathing easier to start, his lungs stop producing liquid and start absorbing it

Throughout most of pregnancy, a baby's lungs produce liquid. At term, they are filled with roughly 100mls of liquid (some of which the lungs have produced and the rest has been supplied by the waters surrounding the baby). Once labour starts, however, the lungs must change to do the opposite; instead of producing liquid they start to absorb it. This is in preparation for a baby taking his very first breath.

If a baby is born vaginally, some of this excess liquid will also be expelled from his lungs when his chest is squeezed during birthing. But a baby born by caesarean section does not get the same squeezing of his chest so he is more likely to need help with his first breath, and to find breathing harder work for some hours after birth. However, if his mother has laboured before the caesarean, his lungs will have already started to absorb some of their surplus fluid.

82 At birth a baby has to make a huge effort to take his first breath

The pressure needed to draw air into the lungs for the first time can be as much effort as it would be for an adult to take 20 breaths all at once. This is because the muscles used for breathing need to pull apart the walls of the lungs that are 'held' together by surface tension.

As soon as a baby has opened his lungs, breathing becomes easier, and the pressure reduces over the following breaths, gradually becoming the same as an adult's. Many babies achieve this feat with just a murmur or two and they don't need to scream as is so often portrayed.

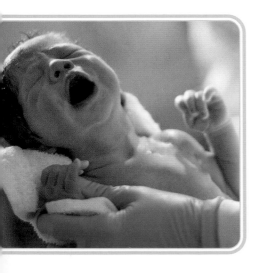

83 After birth a baby can carry out life saving manoeuvres

It has been discovered that a newly born baby, following a drug-free birth, can make his own way from his mother's belly to her breast and start to feed. Thus, a healthy newborn is designed to help himself stay

alive – even if no one else can help him at that time.

A newborn is also designed to help his mother in times of trouble, as the way in which he reaches her breast, is by repeatedly pushing on her belly with his feet. This, as well as breastfeeding, causes his mother's womb to contract and lose less blood.

84 Babies are born equipped with helpful reflexes

A reflex is an automatic response to a particular stimulation, often related to self-protection such as blinking when something comes close to the eye. By birth, a baby has numerous reflexes including some that are unique to that time of life.

The rooting and sucking reflexes help a baby to feed by causing her to turn towards a stroke of her cheek and to open her mouth, and on feeling a nipple (or finger) in her mouth, to start to suck.

The grasp reflex is thought to have arisen in a time when people were hairier, and this helps a baby to hold on to her mother. When something is put into a baby's hand, she will grasp hold of it and, if it is pulled slightly, she will hold on even more tightly. Stroking the back of a baby's closed fist will cause her to open it.

The traction response protects a baby's neck if she is lifted up gently by her hands from a

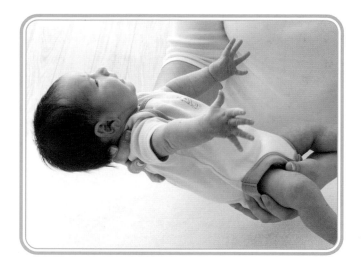

supine position. In response to this action, a baby will draw her head up and then rest it on her chest.

When a baby is surprised by a sudden sound or movement, she reacts with a startle reflex believed to be designed to frighten off a predator, and attract the attention of a parent at a time when safety or comforting are needed. She flings open her arms, legs and hands and then quickly draws them in.

85 A newborn can recognise her mother's face

A baby is born with all the necessary senses and brain development to tell her mother's face apart from other women's faces after just four hours, if she is in direct contact with her mother after the birth. Experiments also show that a baby has the ability to show her preference for her mother's face over that of other women. If she is given a dummy that controls which face she sees, by the speed at which she sucks, she will quickly adjust her rate of sucking in favour of the picture of her mother's face.

86 ...and also familiar voices and respond to them

A newly born infant will recognise the voices of people close to her mother, such as other family members she lives with, and on hearing them speak, she will turn her head in their direction. She is

particularly attentive to human speech but will also react to other sounds. Loud unfamiliar noises will make her startle and are likely to cause her distress evidenced by crying. A baby needs to have become used to specific loud or sudden noises by seven months in the womb for her not to find them distressing after birth. However, some studies have advised that it is possible for babies to suffer hearing damage if loud sounds are heard in the womb.

The Newborn

87 Special cells make it possible for newborns to imitate expressions

Babies are born with special cells that make it possible for them to copy facial expressions, seen just once, by using exactly the same muscles in the same way in their own face. The moment a baby is born and opens his eyes, if he can see a face in focussing distance – about 20 centimetres, or the distance from a baby cradled in his mother's arms to her face – he can start to learn from it.

88 ...and they can reach out to touch their mother's face

It has been discovered, by slowing down videos of newborns, that they can reach out to touch the face of the person holding them. This is not a reflex movement and requires a high level of coordination between the eyes, areas of the

brain and the arm muscles. It is not something that all babies attempt.

After birth, babies are keen to communicate with people close to them and this is just one of the ways they might use. They often try to get a good look at the person holding them, particularly when they are talked to. People frequently don't realise this is what they are doing, as, for them to get the best view, they have to look more from the corner of their eyes than straight on. Closeness and interchange like this after birth help the hormonal changes that are natural at this time in baby, mum and dad and thus enhance communication and feelings of love and affection.

The Newborn

89 A newborn has an incredible sense of smell

A baby is far more sensitive to odours than an adult. At one day old, a baby can smell the difference between a breast pad worn by her mother and one worn by another woman.

In studies, babies have shown their preference for their mother's scent by turning more frequently towards her pad, even when it is moved from side to side. It seems it is the mother's scent a baby is drawn to rather than the milk.

The attraction is less strong in bottlefed babies, though this is thought to be because they tend to spend less time with their face cuddled against their mother's skin.

90 ...and all her teeth in bud form and more bones than an adult

Both the milk teeth and the 'adult' teeth are under the baby's gums waiting for the right time to mature and emerge. The newborn's bones are also formed, but are different to an adults' as babies have almost 100 more. As a baby grows, some of these bones fuse together eventually reducing the number to 206, which is the usual number for an adult.

91 Babies have acutely sensitive skin

Just as touch is the first sense to develop in the womb, so it is the most highly developed in the newly born baby. One million nerve endings enable the newborn to sense touch, temperature and pain. Indeed, relative to size, a baby has more nerves for feeling pain than an adult. Some of these are in the skin and others are deeper in the body. It is now recognised that babies frequently suffer from headaches after a vaginal birth, and pain in the parts of the body they are pulled out by during a caesarean birth. These areas of the body can continue to cause discomfort for a considerable time (see item 55).

92 ... and come in all different sizes

The difference between the lightest and heaviest surviving babies at birth, on record, is a staggering 22 pounds (10 kg). *The Guinness Book of World Records* documents Rumaisa  Rahman, born in Chicago in 2004, as the lightest baby at birth, weighing 8.6 ounces (244 g), and a son born to Carmelina Fedele in Italy in 1955 as the heaviest at 22 pounds 8 ounces (10.3 kg).

93 A baby's birth weight is a more reliable indicator of his chance of developing certain health problems later in life, than his lifestyle

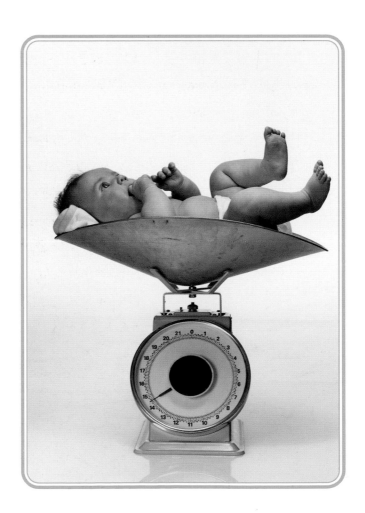

Research by Dr David Barker, Professor of Clinical Epidemiology at the University of Southampton, has confirmed that small babies are most likely to suffer from illnesses, such as heart disease and high blood pressure, decades later. (However, babies that are heavier due to maternal diabetes or other maternal conditions, such as excessive weight gain, do not necessarily benefit from reduced health risks.)

Genes (see item 30) affect a baby's birth weight as does anything, such as smoking, that interferes with him receiving oxygen and nutrients.

The amount of nutrients a woman has in her body in the first weeks of pregnancy (even if it changes radically later) affects the size her baby's body 'designs itself' to grow. Therefore, a woman's diet before she gets pregnant has a significant effect on her child's health. In fact, even the amount of 'food' there was available for her when she was developing in her mother's womb affects her offspring many years later when she herself gets pregnant.

94 By birth, a baby's brain is highly sensitive and responsive to movement

Just inside the head near the ear, is the vestibular system, which tells a baby about movement, particularly rhythmical, of her head or whole body. It is this area of a baby's brain that is involved in her great enjoyment of rocking after birth. Although much of the brain at birth has a lot of maturing still to do, this part is already highly developed. In the womb, a baby gets used to being rocked by her mother's movements such as when walking, swaying or dancing.

The vestibular system is connected to learning and intelligence. When rhythmical movement is perceived, it helps the rest of a baby's brain to become coordinated and move out of a 'disorganised' state, which happens when a baby is very distressed. In other words, it helps to comfort a baby and bring her into a state of quiet alertness, where learning can take place. If the rocking continues, a baby gradually becomes drowsy and falls asleep, unless she has some discomfort such as feeling hungry.

For thousands of years, babies have been carried for most of the first months after birth, thus giving their

vestibular system many hours of rocking each day! The many types of equipment – cradles, mini hammocks, baby swings – created to provide it are testament to its effectiveness but when a baby is rocked in someone's arms, the physical contact is even more comforting.

A baby's enjoyment of bouncing, swinging and rocking will continue into childhood and be evident in playground visits.

The Newborn

95 A whole new world is created with each baby

Each person sees and experiences the world differently and that is true of babies as well. As a result of his unique combination of genes, womb environment and birth, a baby's world is an individual one. For example, he may be especially warmly

welcomed because he looks just like his dad, feel comforted because he hears a TV theme tune familiar from when he was in utero or lethargic because his mum was given lots of analgesic during labour. How he's looked after and in what surroundings also contribute to making a new baby's world completely unique to him.

96 Giving birth is the shortest amount of time in which a woman will naturally lose the greatest amount of weight

The average weight loss post birth is 11 pounds plus whatever is lost on account of the hard physical work of labour. The average length of labour is nine hours, but this varies hugely, with some women labouring for less than one hour and others for over 20.

97 It takes months to 'recover' after pregnancy and birth

On a physical level, the bones that move during pregnancy can take a year to return to their normal places and stretched muscles also take months to re-shape. It'll be months, too, before the minerals that have been given up to the baby are fully replenished.

On an emotional level, it can take years for parents to assimilate the experience and outcome of pregnancy and birth. Women report having strong emotions about their experience of giving birth, certainly in the days that follow, but often still decades later, too.

In the days immediately after birth it is not just the mum and baby who experience a shift in hormones, which are connected to emotional states, dads do, too. However, mums and babies undergo a further big change, which usually happens at three to four days after birth, when pregnancy hormones leave their bodies. As a result, this can be an emotional time.

Even without hormonal changes, intense emotions are only to be expected in the post-natal period as a result of the huge life transformation taking place. In

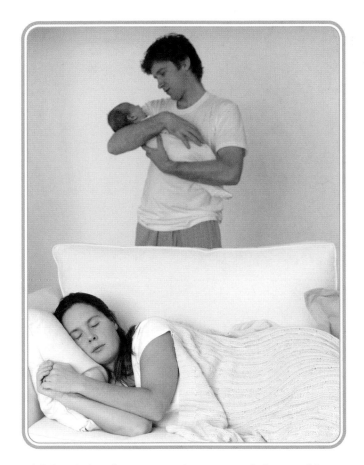

addition, it has been strongly suggested that at this time, too, parents are also reminded of their own birth and early reception, which may prompt still more strong feelings.

Enjoying being together in a tranquil space can help all the hormonal and emotional changes to be assimilated.

98 Babies are designed to help their mums get back into shape after birth

Younger babies encourage their mums to pick them up at virtually all possible opportunities. This, along with the baby's steady weight gain, provides a perfect package for turning mum's fat into muscle. What's more, once a baby is a couple of months old and can be 'used' playfully as a weight, he is able to give encouragement with his delight at being involved in his mum's exercise.

99 A mother may always have a bit of her baby with her

It has recently been discovered that most women who have been pregnant have a small number of their baby's cells in them.

While a baby is in the womb, it seems stem cell transference takes place between the mother and her baby. These cells have the potential to turn into any type of body cell. If they do this, their cell descendants can live for decades in the mother, with her son's or daughter's DNA in them. It works the other way around as well, with over 25% of adults still carrying a few cells from their mother.

100 A mother's milk can be especially life-saving for her baby if he is born prematurely

When a baby is born early, he needs special care in many ways to compensate for the immaturity of his body. His immune system is no exception, and even with the extra attention given to hygiene in neonatal

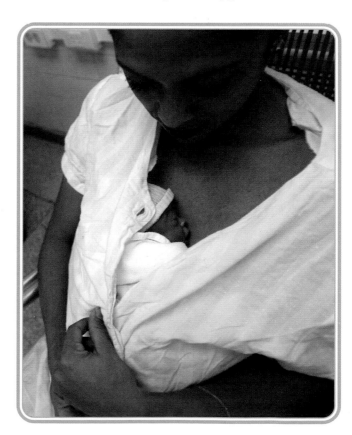

intensive care, premature babies die from infections every year.

Breast milk is a remarkable source of immune strengthening agents including personalised antibodies. It contains lymphocytes and macrophages that 'eat' foreign particles in the body such as bacteria, and neutrophils which create tailor-made antibodies as they are required. Breast milk gives particular protection to a baby's digestive system through antibacterial and antiviral action. However, like any fresh food, processing breast milk changes its value. Freezing it, exposing it to light, putting it in contact with plastic and pasteurising it all reduce its health-giving qualities.

The care of premature babies has advanced beyond recognition in the last decades, yet in two respects it is reverting to age-old practices: the use of beneficial 'kangaroo care', which provides contact with and closeness to another body, and the encouragement of breast milk in their diet.

101 It is possible to get pregnant just three weeks after giving birth

That would mean two babies under one year old!

A woman's menstrual cycle can start back just one week after giving birth, resulting in the release of an egg two weeks later. Full and frequent breastfeeding often delays this, but is no guarantee.

Index

BOOKLIST

Acknowledging What is: Conversations With Bert Hellinger, Bert Hellinger BA, Gabriele Ten Heovel & Colleen Beaumont; Zeig Tucker & Theisen Publishers 1999

Biobehavioral Responses to Stress in Females: Tend-and-Befriend, Not Fight-or-Flight, Shelley Taylor et al; Psychology Review 2000

Birth As We Know It, Elena Tonetti-Vladimirova; e. tonetti 2006

Couvade Syndrome: Male Counterpart to Pregnancy, H Klein; Int. Journal of Psychiatry Med 1991

Early Intelligence How the Brain and the Mind Develop in the First Five Years of Life, Lisa Eliot PhD; Penguin Books 1999

Echoes From the Womb: The Enduring Effects of Prenatal Experience, Ludwig Janus MD; Mattes Verlag 2001

Effects of Experience on Fetal Voice Recognision, Barbara Kisilevsky et al; American Psychological Science May 2003

Embryonic and Early Fetal Development of Human Taste Buds: A Transmission Electron Microscopy Study, Martin Witt & Klaus Reutter; The Anatomical Record December 1996

Essential Anatomy and Physiology in Maternity Care, Linda Wylie BA, MN, RGN, RM, RMT; Elsevier Churchill Livingstone 2000

Factors Influencing Rising Caesarean Section Rates in China Between 1988 and 2008, Xing Lin Feng et al; Bulletin of the World Health Organisation 2012

Feeding and Nutrition in the Preterm Infant, Elizabeth Jones MPhil, RM, RN & Caroline King BSc(Hons), SRD; Elsevier Churchill Livingstone 2005

From Fetus to Child: An Observational and Psychoanalytic Study, Alessandra Piontelli MD; Tavistock/Routledge 1992

From the Dawn of Foetal Senses to Mother-Baby Interaction, Dr Marie-Claire Busnel, Birthlight Trust Launch Conference: Visions of Infant Joy 2006

Human Reproductive Biology 3rd Ed., Richard Jones & Kristin Lopez; Elsevier 2006

Generating Healthy People; Stages in Reproduction Particularly Vulnerable to Xenobiotic Hazards and Nutritional Deficits, Simon House MD, Nutrition and Health, March 2000

Guinness World Records 2010 and 2011, Craig Glenday, Matt Boulton & Ben Way; The Jim Patterson Group 2009, 2010

Langman's Medical Embryology 11th Ed., TW Sadler PhD; Lippincott Williams & Wilkins 2010

Larsen's Human Embryology 4th Ed., Gary Schoenwolf PhD et al, Elsevier 2009

Longitudinal Evidence that Fatherhood Decreases Testosterone in Human Males, Lee Gettler et al, Proceedings of National Academy of Science 2011

Maternal, Fetal and Neonatal Physiology a clinical perspective, Susan Tucker Blackburn PhD, RN, FAAN; Saunders 2003

Mayes Midwifery, Christine Henderson MA, MTD, DPHE, DipN, RN, RM & Sue MacDonald MSc, PGCEA, ADM, RN, RM, ILTM, FETC; Bailliere Tindall 2009

Molecules of Emotion, Candice Pert PhD; Omnia Books 1997

Mothers, Babies and Disease in Later Life, David Barker BSc, PhD, MD, FRCP, FRCOG, FFPHM; BMJ Publishing Group 1994

Myles Textbook for Midwives 14th Ed., Diane Fraser Bed, MPil, PhD, RGN, RM, MTD & Margaret Cooper BA, RGN, RM, MTD; Churchill Livingstone 2003

Multiple Pregnancy: Epidemiology, Gestation and Perinatal Outcome, Isaac Blinckstein MD & Louis Keith MD, PhD; Taylor & Francis 2005

Neonate Movement is Synchronised with Adult Speech: Interactional Participation and Language Acquisition, William Cordon & Louis Sander; Science January 1974

Normal Fetal Motility: An Overview, J.I.P. de Vries & B.F. Fong, Ultrasound in Obs & Gyn, June 2006

Orgasmic Birth The Best Kept Secret, Christine Northrup, MD, FACOG; Sunken Treasure 2008

Pain Research ans Clinical Management; Pain in Neonates and Infants 3rd Ed., KJS Anand MBBS, DPhil, et al, Elsevier 2007

Prenatal Anxiety Predicts Individual Differences in Cortisol in Pre-adolescent Children,

Rates of Caesarean Section: Analysis of Global, Regional and

National Estimates, Ana Betran et al; Paediatric & Perinatal Epidemiology 2007

Reproductive Ritual: The Perception of Fertility in England From the Sixteenth Century to the Nineteenth Century, Angus McLaren; Methuen & Co 1984

Research Overview: Exploring the Role of the Heart in Human Performance, Rollin McCraty PhD; HeartMath Research Centre 1997

The Female Pelvis, Anatomy and Exercises, Blandine Calais-Germain ; Eastland Press 2003

The Heart in the Womb, Amali Lokugamage BSc, MBChB, MD, MSc, FRCOG; Docamali Ltd 2011

The Oxytocin Factor, Tapping the Hormone of Calm, Love and Healing, Kerstin Uvnas Moberg MD, PhD; Pinter & Martin 2011

The Potential of Four-dimensional (4D) Ultrasonography in the Assessment of Fetal Awareness, Asim Kurjak et al; Journal of Perinatal Medicine, June 2006

The Reproductive System at a Glance 3rd ed., Linda Heffner MD, PhD & Danny Schust MD; Wiley –Blackwell 2010

The Unborn Child, Beginning a Whole Life and Overcoming Problems of Early Origin, Roy Ridgeway & Simon House MA; Karnac 2006

With Child: Wisdom and Traditions for Pregnancy, Birth and Motherhood, Deborah Jackson, Chronicle Books 1999

Your Amazing Newborn, Marshall Klaus MD & Phyllis Klaus CSW MFCC; Perseus Books 1999

Yoga for Pregnancy, Françoise Freedman PhD & Doriel Hall; Ward Lock 2005

AUTHOR'S ACKNOWLEDGEMENTS

Firstly, my gratitude goes to my family and friends for all their help and encouragement. In particular, I would like to thank Dr Françoise Freedman, without whom this book might never have materialised and also Romany Buck for her generosity of friendship and wisdom. My thanks go to everyone who has helped, with their enthusiasm and invaluable information, especially Dr Berenice Golding, Dr Ludwig Janus, Simon House, Ursula Berghald, Dr Marilyn Glenville, Dr Amali Lokugamage and Lee Gettler. I would also like to thank all the women, babies and their families that I have worked with and from whom I have learnt so very much. Please visit my website www.afronmonro.com for more information.

PHOTO AND ILLUSTRATION CREDITS

Jules Selmes
Cover images, p63, p103, p120.

Trish Gant
p110, p115.

Corbis Images
p2, p10-11, p12, p14, p16-17, p21, p22, p24-25, p28, p33, p35, p37, p39, p40, p42, p47, p49, p54, p57, p64, p70, p76, p84, p86, p88, p90, p91, p93, p94, p95, p100,

p101, p105, p109, p111, p112, p116, p117, p119, p122, p124.

Getty Images
p13, p55, p67, p68, p78-79, p80, p83, p98, p104, p106, p107.

Science Photo
p19, p29, p32, p36, p44, p50, p59, p62, p73, p77, p82, p96, p97.

Photolibrary
p53.

Professer Stuart Campbell
p46, p52, p58, p61, p69, p74.

Amanda Williams
p48, p56, p75.

Also available from Carroll & Brown to help you enjoy your pregnancy

Pregnancy Week by Week
by Dr. Jane MacDougall

Your ideal companion to the 40+ weeks of pregnancy, this guide contains vital information on how your body changes in pregnancy and your baby develops in utero as well as a handy diary feature that enables you to keep track of doctor and clinic appointments, test dates and fitness and childbirth classes. Its stand-up format and handy size makes it easily portable and able to be viewed from any surface.

ISBN: 978 1 907952 04 3

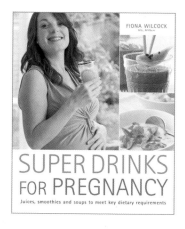

Super Drinks for Pregnancy
by Fiona Wilcock, MSc, RPHNutr

Getting a good supply of essential nutrients is not always easy in pregnancy when one's appetite may be surpressed by an enlarging abdomen or nausea. But many of the vital foodstuffs can be taken in liquid form in easily prepared soups, drinks and juices that are quick to prepare and specially designed to meet a pregnant woman's needs.

ISBN: 978 1 907952 07 4

Sold in high street and online bookshops and at www.carrollandbrown.co.uk